D0192576

Skomer – Portrait of a Welsh Island
Published in Great Britain in 2018
by Graffeg Limited

Written by Jane Matthews copyright © 2018.
Designed and produced by Graffeg Limited
copyright © 2018.

First published by Graffeg in 2007, and then
revised in 2011.

Graffeg Limited, 24 Stradey Park Business
Centre, Mwrwg Road, Llangennech, Llanelli,
Carmarthenshire SA14 8YP Wales UK
Tel 01554 824000 www.graffeg.com

Jane Matthews is hereby identified as the
author of this work in accordance with
section 77 of the Copyrights, Designs and
Patents Act 1988.

A CIP Catalogue record for this book is
available from the British Library.

All rights reserved. No part of this
publication may be reproduced, stored
in a retrieval system or transmitted, in
any form or by any means, electronic,
mechanical, photocopying, recording or
otherwise, without the prior permission of
the publishers.

Cover photograph: Puffin by Dave Boyle.

ISBN 9781912213344

1 2 3 4 5 6 7 8 9

Dedicated to the memory of
Amber Rowlands (1972-2017)

Skomer

Portrait of a Welsh Island

GRAFFEG

Iolo Williams

If I were to choose one Welsh nature reserve that could hold its own against any other reserve, anywhere in the world, it would have to be Skomer.

It is the diamond in the crown jewels of Welsh wildlife and little wonder, therefore, that it attracts thousands of visitors each year.

It holds a third of the world population of Manx Shearwaters, thousands of Puffins, Guillemots and Razorbills, a significant proportion of the Welsh population of Short-eared Owls, the unique Skomer Vole and the seas surrounding the island are amongst the richest in Britain.

There is no doubt that it is a naturalist's paradise and I have been privileged to visit the island on more than 40 occasions over the past 25 years. However, it is not just the wildlife that makes Skomer such a magical place.

The people, too, are very special. I have had the pleasure of walking with a succession of enthusiastic, dedicated and knowledgeable wardens and researchers, learning new facts every single time I go. Their warmth and willingness to help has always made a visit to Skomer that little bit more special.

For anyone who has never visited the island in spring and summer, I would urge you to get out there as soon as you can. It's a unique experience, and one that will remain vivid in the memory for years afterwards.

Iolo Williams, Naturalist, TV presenter, conservationist and writer.

Left: **Tom's House** South-east from Skomer Head lies Tom's House and The Amos, with The Wick beyond. Photo Dave Boyle

Contents

Preface

Moving from north London to Skomer Island was a sea-change of adventure, a gloriously rich way to start my thirties. It was a magical place to live for five years and an unforgettable setting for the first two years of parenthood.

My time on Skomer was made most memorable by the people who cared passionately for it; whether staff, researchers, volunteers or visitors, I was struck by their dedication and zeal. With a toddler on one knee and a laptop on the other I put together this book as a way of telling the story of the island through all our eyes.

Life on the island seems even more incredible from the relatively conventional perch I now live on. My daughter is a teenager and still has a few etched memories of her early years there. Skomer has different wardens but the essence of the place remains exactly the same. Some facts, figures and images have been updated for this edition but the

rest is timeless. I am grateful to all those who contributed to make, and update, this portrait of a unique island.
Jane Matthews, 2018

50% of the royalties from the sale of this book will be donated to The Wildlife Trust of South and West Wales, registered charity number 1091562.

Left: **South Haven in the Mist**
Photo Jane Matthews

Introduction

Skomer Island lies less than a mile off shore from the Marloes Peninsula in Pembrokeshire, yet it is this short span of water that sets the island a world apart from its neighbours.

Free from all land-based predators, Skomer has evolved as its own bustling ecosystem in a unique and spectacular landscape. Covering over 300 hectares this treeless island is world famous for its breeding colonies of seabirds.

More than 25,000 Puffins crowd the cliff-tops; the largest colony in southern Britain, and breeding birds can be seen at close quarters throughout June and July fluttering in with beaks full of fish for their chicks. The island also boasts over 300,000 pairs of the Manx Shearwater; a curious bird that only returns to land under the cloak of darkness. Its raucous call was thought by sailors to be the cries of lost souls at sea and provides a unique soundtrack to a night on the island. With thousands of shearwaters literally dropping in from the night sky during their long nesting season, the island is transformed into a strange and mystical world; the stuff of fantasy.

Many other rare and dazzling species of fauna and flora abound on Skomer and as the seasons wheel, so too revolve its colours, smells and sounds. From the psychedelic purple of the Bluebell blanket that quivers over the island in late May to the russet-red of the autumn Bracken. From whirring Guillemots to cronking Ravens, Skomer is an exotic bazaar of the natural world.

Woven into this wilderness is man's presence on the island. Settlement remains date back to the Iron Age, giving the island its status as one of the best preserved Scheduled Ancient Monuments in Britain. Shadows of a more recent farming history lie at the centre of the island where the farm buildings still stand. The imposing ruined farmhouse is a sober relic of the harsh – but periodically prosperous – time for the island's farming population that extended through to the mid twentieth century.

Skomer is now a National Nature Reserve, owned by the Natural Resources and managed by the Wildlife Trust of South and West Wales. A small team of staff, researchers and volunteers populate the island from March to November each year, living in tune with the island and its resources. With no mains water or mains electricity, no landlines, shops or cars, living on Skomer is a story in itself, and one best told through the images and anecdotes of those who love it.

Left: **Towards Skomer from The Deer Park**
Photo Mike Alexander

Jane Matthews

"...See my child, how remarkable is the Island of Skomer!
Come with me, I will show you every cranny of its outer shore".
Hilaire Belloc, *The Cruise of the Nona* (1925)

Right: **Skomer and Middleholm** 'Skomer' derives from 'Skalmey', the Viking name for the island: Skalm (meaning short sword, reflecting the island's shape) and ey (island). Vikings invaded the Welsh coast in 850 AD. Photo Juan Brown

Left: **South Haven and The Neck** Erosion
of softer sedimentary rock has created a
narrow isthmus separating the main
island from The Neck to the east.
Photo Chris Perrins

The Wildlife Trust of South and West Wales

The Wildlife Trust of South and West Wales is a charitable organisation that manages 90 nature reserves, from Cardiff and Caerphilly in the east of Wales to Ceredigion and Pembrokeshire in the west, including four of the west Wales islands. These nature reserves form a land holding equal to approximately 4,500 acres; 16 lie within Special Areas of Conservation and Special Protection Areas; nine are National Nature Reserves (NNRs); 48 are Sites of Special Scientific Interest (SSSIs) and five are Scheduled Ancient Monuments.

Whilst many of the reserves are located within some of the most rural areas of the country, a proportion are found within the heart of industrial Wales and some are located within, or close to, severely deprived inner city areas. The Trust manages Skomer Island along with St. Margaret's and Cardigan Islands and Skokholm (the island two miles south of Skomer) which it owns. The Trust's work is carried out by a team of both permanent and seasonal staff, who in turn rely on dedicated groups of volunteers without whom this work would be difficult to deliver.

The Wildlife Trust of South and West Wales is one of 47 local Wildlife Trusts that, combined, manage 2,300 reserves across the whole of the UK. With more than 800,000 members it is the largest UK voluntary organisation dedicated to conserving a diverse range of natural habitats and species, fostering sustainable living and inspiring a love of the natural world.

Information correct at the time of writing. For more information and educational resources please visit **www.welshwildlife.org**

Left: **Razorbill (*Alca torda*)** Razorbills nest on Skomer in internationally important numbers. Photo Dave Boyle

Flying hopefully into the night, leaving our cares behind..

by Matthew Parris

A PALE HALF MOON was up, which was a pity. Far below we could hear a gentle Atlantic swell licking the rocks. From a cave at the cliffs' feet came the bark of a cow seal guarding her pup. The Pembrokeshire coast glimmered across a strait silvered by moonlight. The slightest of breezes stirred the Bracken...

...The reason it was a pity about the moon was that a fledgling Manx Shearwater prefers pitch black before he ventures out. Until now he has lived almost without light. Below ground in his burrow his parents' single egg was laid, guarded and incubated for nearly two months before he hatched; since then he has spent ten weeks growing fat and fluffy in the dark.

His only intimation of a world beyond the burrow has been the rush of wings outside as father or mother fly in – always at night, the darker and stormier the better – with gurgling, cackling shrieks and a delivery of liquid fish paste.

He cannot walk. He cannot fly. Of sun and sunshine he knows nothing, save that on some strange unconscious level in his tiny brain, danger and light are associated – sunlight in which his and his parents' merciless predator, the Great Black-backed Gull, can spot and target a defenceless, feathered fluffball flapping and stumbling in the Skomer Bracken. Even the weak beam of my torch now disconcerts him.

And on that same unconscious level he knows something else; that very soon – perhaps tomorrow – he must fly to Brazil. Tonight he must learn to fly.

The Manx Shearwater is one of the wonders of the world... about half of the world's entire population of this diminished but now stable species breeds on tiny Skomer (about a mile wide) and the even tinier island of Skokholm nearby.

Since rats drove shearwaters from the Calf of Man, "Manx" has become a misnomer. Everything about this bird confuses. Sailors mistook the adults' night cry – like a demented chicken's –

Above: **Pole Star** On a clear night above the Trig Point the stars are captured, in a long exposure photograph, revolving around the Pole Star. It is this night sky which is thought to form the basis of the shearwater's spectacular navigational system that leads them on their migratory passage to and from South America.
Photo Brian Hewitt

Above: **Manx Shearwater (*Puffinus puffinus*) Fledgling** With legs set so far back on their bodies shearwaters must launch themselves from the highest possible point for the best chance of take-off. The first time they get airborne will mark the start of their 7000 mile journey to South America. Photo Mike Alexander

for the screams of souls in torment. Some fool dubbed the bird a puffin, which it never was, and to this day its Latin name, Puffinus puffinus, bewilders students, while the French still call it the English Puffin. Until relatively recently its migrations – like its part-subterranean lifestyle – have been wrapped in mystery.

No newcomer to the species would guess that the chick – swollen by a diet of oily baby food into a big, fluff-upholstered butterball, outweighing its parents – is even related to the slim-winged, black-and-white flying ace of the Atlantic, streaking across the oceans in search of sardines to disgorge into the open beak waiting back in the burrow. Over a life of up to half a century one bird may fly further than to the Moon and back.

I am learning such things. With me on Skomer to help to teach was the permanent warden stationed there by the Wildlife Trust of South and West Wales, Juan Brown. We tied up at the jetty after lunch. Juan directed us to the ruins of an old farm... There are no roads or cars and we walked a grassy track through rocks and Bracken, carrying sleeping bags... and food. A few gulls patrolled. Rabbits gambolled. All was quiet and sunny. Nothing – nothing except the honeycomb of burrows everywhere you looked, and the occasional heap of feathers around

a gull-pecked fledgling corpse - alerted the rambler to a parallel universe beneath our boots. Inches underground lay a nursery city, the Rome of the shearwater world. Tens of thousands of hearts were beating down there, hundreds of thousands of small hopefuls, new-feathered, were awaiting their big moment. Their big moment was soon.

At dusk my producer and I walked the half-mile across to the warden's cottage, to interview him. Juan Brown knew his stuff and sounded keen, though he must have heard the questions a thousand times. I asked how fledglings know September is the time to come out of their burrows by night and learn to fly? Their parents simply leave, he said. They fly off to South America. They just have. A few days later the chicks scramble from their burrows. Nobody is sure why.

How, I asked, do the young birds know the way to South America? Nobody is sure of that, either. Some think the bird's brain responds the Earth's magnetic field, but the great ornithologist Ronald Lockley, who lived and worked on nearby Skokholm more than 60 years ago, proved that shearwaters orient themselves best when the sky (night or day) is clear. He had two shearwaters crated up and sent to Boston in America. They arrived back in their Skokholm burrows – their exact burrows – before the letter advising of their release. How, he asked, did they do this?

Go into the night on a starry night. There is only one place on Earth from which, at (say) midnight on Tuesday, September 16, a clear sky at night will appear as it does from where you are standing – and that is where you now are. If you always knew the date and time, and if you could access a complete set of starmaps for every time and place, then you could locate yourself by selecting the map which matched the sky you see. This, it is thought, is what migrating birds may do.

But this navigational system must be pegged to a point of reference: the burrow from which the young bird first emerges – and to which, after six years feeding and maturing – he will return to breed. So, stumbling and staring around outside his front door, he is locking onto the sky. For the rest of his life all flight-paths will lead from and to this point, this starry map above one tiny hole in the surface of one tiny island in one tiny corner of the great Atlantic Ocean.

"Follow me," said Juan Brown, "now it's dark, and we'll walk up to the best area for burrows."

Something had happened to the footpath we had walked down at twilight.

It was littered with baby shearwaters. You would at first have thought these birds were dying – sick, perhaps, or poisoned.

Each was flopping desperately around. They could not stand; when they tried walking they would fall forward onto their breasts. Their legs were too far back to balance so they kept toppling, beak-in-the-dust.

"Having their legs set back," said Juan, "is the perfect design for pursuing fish underwater."

We reached the top of the knoll. I tried switching off our torch. It took time for my eyes to adjust to the dark. When they did, the sight was amazing. It was as if the undergrowth had come alive with pigeon-sized, two-tone, black-and-white fledglings. A few still had patches of butterball down but most had lost it.

Spreading out their wings – long, black, slim, curved and beautiful – they tried to balance. Some were crawling up rocks, cheeping, beating their wings to give them lift, clawing with webbed feet at the rock, teetering on the top, then taking off for exploratory flights which always ended in a painful and undignified crash into the Bracken.

"But they'll learn fast," said Juan, as one more advanced than his peers whirred a full 20 yards down the hill, then came a cropper.

Two chicks were necking affectionately. For all those months underground each may have thought himself the only chick in the world, alone but for the parental beak with its fishpaste meal.

"They mate for life," said Juan.

Everywhere you looked, dark shapes floundered around. On every rock a teetering chick clambered for possession and a launch pad. The whole island, to every horizon, was alive with them. We stood and wondered for an hour.

"You should have been here before the parents left," said Juan. "The noise is amazing".

He explained that on arrival from South America the breeding pairs float just offshore in great rafts of birds, waiting until nightfall. Then, under the cover of the dark, they dive straight in, each for precisely the nest from which they came.

When the egg is laid the parents take it in turns to incubate, and later to fetch food. But they come in only at night – the darker and stormier the better – shrieking to their chick, from whom they always seem to be able to identify from the thousands of others.

Returning to our cabin around midnight I slept peacefully but awoke in the small hours and hearing flapping, walked out into the dark.

All the stars were out. The Milky Way was clear and strong. I stood there alone for a long time. Apart from the apprentice flyers clawing, crashing and flip-flopping in every direction, I was alone beneath a vast sky. A cold breeze hinted at an approaching autumn. As I stood, a young shearwater lurched over my foot – then began to climb my leg, his wings beating. To him I suppose I was just another rock.

What did he know of the journey which lay ahead? He may still be on his travels when mine are over.

I felt as I stood there a solitary and privileged witness to a supremely important moment in the life not only of individuals but of a species. Beneath the canopy of the stars, something immense and timeless was stirring...

Garland
Stone

Double
Cliff

Payne's Rock

Payne's Ledge

Waybench

Bull Hole

Saunders Fist

The Table

North Pond

Green Pond

Landin
Place

Anvil Rock

Public hide

North
Castle

The Spit

Harold
Stone

Well
Meadow

The
Farm

Calves
Park

West Park

ℹ

Pigstone Bay

Marble Rocks

Abyssinia

South
Field

South
Park

New
Park

Shearing
Hays

Warden's
House

The
Pigstone

Rabbit
Exclosure

West
Pond

Young
Ground

Gorse
Hill

Captain Kites

South
Stream
Valley

Seal
Hole

Skomer
Head

South Pond

Public hide

Moory Mere

Welsh
Way

Tom's
House

Wick
Stream

Wick Ridge

South Haven

The Basin

The Wick

Wick Valley

High Cliff

South Plateau

Mew Stone

N

0.5 mile

0.8 km

Broad Sound

Key

	Trails
🚹🚺 ⓘ	Toilets & Information
	Curlews
	Puffin colonies
	Cliff nesting seabirds
	Gull colonies
	Short-eared Owls
	Grey Seals
	Porpoises

St Brides Bay

rth Haven

Rye Rocks

Protheroe's
Dock

The Lantern

The Neck

**Little
Sound**

Middleholm

le Bay

Tusker Rock

Wooltack Point

**Skomer
Embarkation
Point**
● Martin's
Haven

Deer Park

Mainland

Jack Sound

Black Stones

Deadman's Bay

Pitting Gales Point

The Bench

Skomer map   23

Seasonal timeline

	March	April	May	June
Puffins		Puffins return — Nest building and egg laying		Chicks hatch, adults with fish
Razorbills		Razorbills courting — Egg laying		Chicks hatch — Chicks fledge
Guillemots		Guillemots courting — Egg laying		Chicks hatch — Chicks fledge
Manx Shearwater	Manx Shearwaters return to land — Egg laying			Chicks hatch
Chough	Choughs all year round			
Grey Seal	Grey Seals			
Grey Seal pups				
Bluebells			Early flowering — Peak flowering — Late flowering	
Red Campion			Early flowering — Flowering	

July	August	September	October	November
Chicks fledge	Adults leave			

Adults leave

Fledglings exercise then leave

Early pups

Grey Seal pups

Water

The waters around Skomer are protected and have been designated a Marine Conservation Zone. The warm flow of the Gulf Stream mixes with colder northern waters to create this rich marine environment. Surrounded by such a lavish food source, and protected from predators like the fox, rat and weasel, the island's bird populations can thrive.

Clouds Over Jack Sound Looking west to Skomer with Skokholm to the south. Currents and eddies in Jack Sound – and Little Sound to the west – can be deceptively strong. Photo Juan Brown

Jack Sound runs fast and furious between Skomer and the mainland and has at times throughout the ages been a perilous hazard to man and beast. Prince, Skomer's last working horse, made the one-way journey to the island, swimming the Sound in 1947, and remained for the rest of his days. Evidence of an older cattle route worn into the rock emerges from the sea at the island's most easterly tip, which suggests animals were regularly brought to the island under their own steam. Below sea-level the wreck of The Lucy provides some of Britain's most spectacular diving. The ship, laden with carbide, hit rocks in the Sound in 1967 and came to rest on the sea-bed forty metres down at the entrance to North Haven.

The island welcomes visitors between April and the end of September with a usual limit of 250 per day. By October, weather fronts and rough seas can keep the islanders cut off for days – sometimes weeks – at a time.

Above: **Warm Welcome** Ed and Bee
became wardens of Skomer in 2013
and are resident between March and
December each year. Photo Robert Bush
Left: **Skomer Mural** by Rory McCann.
Photo WTSWW
Far left: **Approaching Skomer** The
crossing from Martin's Haven to Skomer
takes just 15 minutes and provides the
ideal opportunity, at the right time of year,
to spot porpoises, seabirds and seals
along the way. Photo Richard Brown

The open arms of North Haven form the gateway to this offshore wilderness. Managing the island requires a fine balance; allowing public access without compromising the very wildlife which makes it so special.

Left: **Visitors Landing on Skomer**
A steep bank of steps greets the visitor to Skomer but, once at the top, the island's plateau is gentle and the walk is relatively easy. A route around the island takes approximately three hours, at a leisurely pace. Photo Jeff Morgan

Above: **Kenny Gainfort** skippered the Dale Princess for over 20 years. Photo Jane Matthews

Left: **Gutting Mackerel** A quiet moment on the Dale Princess gives co-skipper Karl Wonnacott time to prepare his dinner. Photo Bob Ball

Below: **Feeding Frenzy** Over 36,000 pairs of Gannets breed on Grassholm, seven miles west of Skomer. A large bird with black wing-tips and a yellow-buff head, the Gannet can be seen plunge-diving for fish, often amongst feeding porpoises. Seen here with Manx Shearwaters out at sea during the day. Photo Lyndon Lomax

Seabirds reign over these grey-green waters, wholly dependent on the ecosystems within.

Above: **Fulmar (Fulmaris glacialis)**
Skomer's population of Fulmars rose from just four pairs in 1960 to over 700 pairs in the nineties, as part of a southerly spread of the species throughout the British Isles. Photo Dave Boyle

The protection and study of this fragile ecology is essential. Future changes in sea temperature could have a dramatic effect on the health of these waters and every species it supports.

Left: **Dive Preparation** As well as education and the protection of the coastal environment, the work of the Marine Conservation Zone staff involves many hours of close monitoring below sea level. Photo Jennifer Jones (MCZ)

Above: **North Haven** Dense seaweed forests waft in the swell of the shallower waters in North Haven. Photo David Miller

After Pembrokeshire's disastrous *Sea Empress* oil spill of 1995 recovery of the ecosystems above and below the waves has been meticulously monitored by a dedicated team responsible for this Marine Conservation Zone.

Right: **Sea Fan monitoring** The Pink Sea Fan (Eunicella verrucosa) is a coral more commonly found in warmer Mediterranean waters, its northernmost stronghold is the Skomer Marine Conservation Zone. It is one of few marine species protected by law. Over 100 colonies are monitored annually at sites around Skomer, photographs are taken and the condition of each fan is recorded. Photo Rohan Holt (MCZ)

Superbly camouflaged,
this rare sea slug has only
occasionally been recorded
in the Skomer Marine
Conservation Zone.

Left: **Sea Fan Nudibranchs (*Tritonia
nilsodherni*)** Nudibranchs are commonly
known as sea slugs. They are all
carnivores and most have a very selective
choice of food. This nudibranch feeds
only on the Pink Sea Fan and has evolved
to perfectly mimic its polyps.
Photo Mark Burton (MCZ)

Free-floating plankton are paralysed by the stinging tentacles of jellyfish, passed to the mouth and then digested in the central stomach.

Compass Jellyfish (Chrysaora hysoscella)
These majestic creatures can be found throughout the MCZ in the summer months.
Photo Rob Gibbs (MCZ)

Around The Mew Stone deep gullies are found below the sea surface. Water is forced through them in strong surges and only marine life with a good hold will survive.

Left: **Gooseberry Sea Squirts (*Dendrodoa grossularia*)** The Gooseberry Sea Squirt thrives in this turbulent undersea environment forming large carpets on the rocks and filtering the plankton-rich water. Photo Blaise Bullimore (MCZ)

Above: **Crayfish (*Palinurus elegans*)** Crayfish and lobsters are predators on the rocky reefs. Large animals are rarely seen in the MCZ as commercial fishing continues to remove these creatures from the food chain. Unless fishing in the MCZ stops we will never know a truly natural marine environment. Photo Kate Lock (MCZ)

Left: **Dahlia Anemone (*Urticina felina*)**
Flower-like anemones are actually
predators equipped with stinging
tentacles ready to capture food.
Anemones come in many forms, sizes and
colour; 40 species have been recorded
in the Reserve. Photo Blaise Bullimore
(MCZ)

Left below: **Serrated Wrack (*Fucus
serratus*)** As seaweeds become covered
by the tide they are supported by the
water and spring back to life. The sunlight
streams through the shallow waters
allowing them to photosynthesise.
Photo Vicki Howe (MCZ)

Below: **Male Cuckoo Wrasse (*Labrus
mixtus*)** Cuckoo Wrasse are protogynous
hermaphrodites, meaning they are all
born as females but can become males
when a dominant male disappears.
Photo Blaise Bullimore (MCZ)

Left: **Jewel Anemone**
(***Corynactis viridis***) These
underwater jewels are only a
centimetre wide but will form
large sheets of thousands of
individuals. There are many
colour varieties, including
this 'rhubarb and custard'
combination. They reproduce by
cloning, with parent anemones
splitting in two. Photo Kate Lock
(MCZ)

Right: **The Lucy** The Dutch
coaster *The Lucy* ran aground
in Jack Sound on 14th February
1967. It then re-floated and
drifted just outside North Haven
where it sank in 40 metres
of water. The wreck is rich in
marine life; Ghost Anemones
(*Metridium senile*) and Elegant
Anemones (*Sagartia elegans*)
smother the mast and ladder.
Photo Blaise Bullimore (MCZ)

Skomer's Puffin population is the largest in southern Britain with over 25,000 birds returning to breed annually between late March and the end of July.

Puffin (*Fratercula artica*) The Puffin's design is a trade off between flight and diving underwater. Like other auks their bones are heavier than most birds, enabling them to dive to depths of 60 metres. Photo David Miller

Fast and exuberant, the spectacular display of dolphins is a rare but magical sight; leaping and swerving like hooked needles sewing their way through the water.

Above: **Common Dolphins (*Delphinus delphis*)** While porpoises are seen frequently around the coast dolphins are more elusive and generally remain further out to sea. However, in recent years, pods of up to 300 Common Dolphins have been recorded in St. Brides Bay on several occasions during the summer months. Photos Lyndon Lomax

Tankers in the Storm Clouds Beyond the Marine Conservation Zone St. Brides Bay is a holding ground for oil tankers from around the world, waiting to load or offload their cargos at the refineries of Milford Haven. Photo Amber Rowlands

Landscape

Skomer's rock is about 440 million years old and would have been cut off from the mainland by rising sea levels after the last Ice Age. It is essentially volcanic, supporting huge populations of seabirds on cliffs that stand 60 metres high in some places. A deep soil cap over the top of the island provides the perfect habitat for the thousands upon thousands of ground-nesting seabirds that return each year to breed.

Right: **Looking East to Welsh Way from The Neck** Pillows of Thrift bind the fragile terrain above Castle Bay, left to the Rabbits after the ground-nesting seabirds have gone at the end of each season.
Photo Jane Matthews

Left: **Thrift (*Armeria maritima*)** Wick Basin. Above: **The Wick** Flowering Thrift, or Sea Pink, explodes like mini fireworks around Skomer's coast in spring and seabirds return to swarm the rocky shores. Photos Dave Boyle

A human presence on the island dates back between two and five thousand years when the population may have numbered up to 200. Walled fields and settlement remains mark this ancient restructuring of the landscape, but arguably Man's most significant impact was the introduction of the Rabbit in the fourteenth century. Brought to the island to be farmed for food and fur the Rabbits remained long after their economic importance dwindled and today the island is landscaped by the 10,000 or so now running wild. Their grazing pressure has shaped the island's flora particularly by promoting the Bracken, which in turn provides cover for the Bluebell that normally grows in shady woodland. Their burrows provide convenient ready-made homes for the Puffins and shearwaters.

In 2005 a major rebuilding project started on the island to create improved accommodation and visitor services. Work was structured around the breeding season of the birds to avoid disturbance and in October the Warden's House, which had perched amongst the Puffins at North Haven for nearly fifty years, was flattened to make way for a new, improved facility.

Far left: **Approaching The Amos at Dawn** Photo Jane Matthews

Left: **Sea Campion (*Silene uniflora*)**
In spring the island's coastal banks turn white as the sweet-scented Sea Campion blooms. Great swathes of flowers quiver in the whipping wind. Photo Richard Brown

Right: **Bracken (*Pteridium aquilinum*)**
Bracken smothers the island in summer. The leaves and shoots, poisonous to Rabbits, are eaten by the unique Skomer Vole. Photo Tim Guilford

Whether below ground or on the cliff ledges Skomer's landscape functions as one huge breeding platform for the many species of seabird that return year on year.

Above left: **Puffin Feeding Chick Below Ground**

Middle: **Puffin Landing**

Left: **Kittiwake (*Rissa tridactyla*)** Kittiwakes, like other gulls, may lay a clutch of up to three eggs, but Puffins (along with the other auks, shearwaters and petrels) only lay one. With this slow reproduction rate over a long lifespan the Puffin must provide a constant supply of fresh fish for its single investment.

Right: **The Wick**
Photos Mike Alexander, Brian Hewitt, Dave Boyle, Chris Perrins

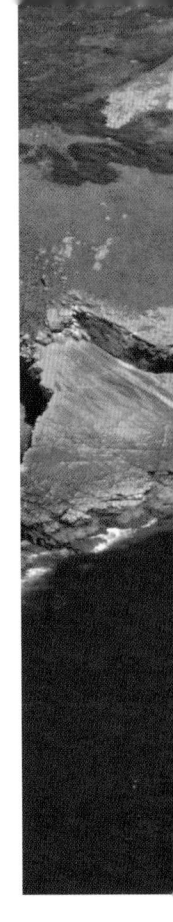

Birds are not the only ones
to enjoy this unique offshore
environment and man has
an integral part to play in
its future.

Left: **Sea Watching** Skomer attracts up to 16,000 visitors a year. However, the overwhelming sense of space remains and it is easy to lose the crowd.
Photo Jeff Morgan

Above: **HQ** The original Warden's House was built with the help of the RAF in 1959 and presided over North Haven for 46 years. An updated building of the same footprint was completed in spring 2007.
Photo Richard Brown

Left: **Demolition of the old Warden's House**
Photos Juan Brown, Jane Matthews

Above: **Warden's House and research accommodation** The new improved building boasts solar and wind-powered systems providing hot water and electricity. Photo Jason Moss

The practicalities of farming the island were complicated enough but it was the harsh winter of 1946-47 that spelled the end for Reuben Codd. After a disastrous potato season the economics of farm life became unrealistic and the island was sold to the Nature Conservancy in 1958.

Left and below: **Renovations at The Old Farm** The original farm house at the centre of the island is thought to have been built around 1700, and the outbuildings were added much later. A loft running the length of the large barn housed the farm workers with horses stabled below. The newly renovated building provides accommodation for researchers and up to 16 paying guests. Photos Birgitta Büche and David Milborrow

Above: **Bluebells (*Hyacinthoides non-scripta*)** In May the island is awash with a quivering haze of purple. Bluebells are a possible relic of previous woodland cover, but today Bracken provides a surrogate canopy as it grows up later in the season. Photo Jane Matthews

Left: **Iron Age Roundhouse** Located near The Wick this human dwelling is thought to date from the early Iron Age, although some believe it may even be neolithic due to a more rectangular look than other round houses. Water would have been collected from South Stream nearby and the surrounding land used

for rough grazing and fuel. The remains of what are thought to be ovens or food stores are built into field boundaries nearby. Photo Jane Matthews

Above: **South Stream Cliff** Layers of volcanic rock provide ledges for a host of seabirds. Photo Dave Boyle

Left: **Castle Bay, Looking East** Over Skomer's volcanic base a deep soil cap provides the ideal habitat for burrow-nesting seabirds.
Photo Jane Matthews

Below: **South Stream Valley**
Photo Bob Ball

The island is landscaped by the Rabbits that have populated Skomer since their introduction in the fourteenth century.

Left: **Bluebells at Dawn** Photo Jane Matthews
Above: **Rabbit (*Oryctolagus cuniculus*)**
The vegetation on the island is shaped by the grazing Rabbits. An outbreak of Myxomatosis caused a population crash in late 2006 but was followed by exceptional display of flowering plants in 2007. Photo Dave Boyle

Arguably the most impressive cliff on Skomer,
The Wick's basalt ledges and earthy cap support
a bustling seabird city.

The Wick Photo Alison Hayes

Populations

Day and night throughout the summer months the island is host to a riotous carnival of breeding seabirds; nearly 20,000 Guillemots, over 5,000 Razorbills, more than 10,000 Puffins and up to 128,000 pairs of Manx Shearwaters. A fragile network of tunnels extends deep into the island's crust, at the end of each a cosy hole shields a Puffin, shearwater (or a family of rabbits) from hungry gulls above.

Right: **Congregating Puffins at South Haven** During the breeding season huge crowds of Puffins congregate on the cliff tops at dusk. Communication with neighbours is important and such gatherings are busy with birds head-jerking, bill-tapping and groaning at each other. Photo Dave Boyle

On every cliff ledge and crevice Guillemots pack tightly together like skittles, each pair with a single egg between them balanced precariously on warm feet. All these seabirds can live for many years and return to land, after months at sea, to breed. Other, rarer species are also found amid the breeding mayhem. The Skomer Vole, a sub-species of the mainland Bank Vole, thrives on the island's Bracken but is hunted by the Short-eared Owl, gliding low across the valleys. Peregrine, Chough and Curlew are all resident throughout the year.

As the summer ends and the seabirds leave, the island's Grey Seal population takes the spotlight. Between August and December over 200 pups are born in caves and on beaches around the island. Like seabirds, the seals generally breed each year and can live well into their thirties.

All these populations are scrupulously monitored by the human population – a core of two or three who are joined by volunteers, researchers and visitors throughout the summer months as the island reaches the peak of activity. By late autumn however, as weather fronts shift and the Bracken dies back, Skomer is left to regain its solitary presence once more.

Left: **Grey Seal (*Halichoreus grypus*) – Pup** Grey Seal pups usually weigh about 14kg when born and are expected to triple their weight in the first three weeks of life. Photo Jane Matthews

Grey seals have been recorded diving to 70m and can possibly go deeper, but they usually feed in shallow coastal waters. Adults breed between August and December.

Left: **Grey Seal, Cow and Pup** Until weaned at approximately three weeks old the Grey Seal pup will live solely off its mother's high-fat milk. Feeding herself up before giving birth, the mother lives off her reserves until the pup is weaned, losing weight as quickly as the pup puts it on. She remains close by, feeding her pup several times a day. Photo Jane Matthews

Puffins Male Puffins generally have slightly longer and deeper bills than females, and in both sexes the grooves on the bill develop as the bird ages. These grooves are thought to be integral to their mating strategies. Photos Bob Ball, Dave Boyle, Jane Matthews

The Puffin, monochrome throughout the winter months, reaches full colour in time for the breeding season with vermillion legs and a distinct arrow-like beak of orange, yellow and blue.

Acrobats, dancers and clockwork clowns star in Skomer's circus of birdlife.

Above and left: **Chough (*Pyrrhocorax pyrrhocorax*)** The Chough has broad 'fingered' wings, scarlet legs and bill. Pembrokeshire is one of the strongholds of this distinctive member of the crow family. Three to four pairs nest on Skomer. Photos Dave Boyle

Right: **Puffin Chick** In July young Puffins venture out of their burrows to limber up, before leaving the island under the cloak of darkness at six weeks old. Photo Brian Hewitt.
Below: **Manx Shearwaters at Sea** Photo Ben Dean

Left: **Razorbill**

Above: **Razorbill Chick** Over 5,000 Razorbills nest on ledges and in rocky crevices around the coast. Each egg is incubated for approximately 35 days. As with the Guillemot, the Razorbill chick leaps from the cliff at less than three weeks old and is taken out to sea by its father. Photos Dave Boyle

Above: **Short-eared Owl (*Asio flammeus*)**
Short-eared Owls, which nest on the
island, can often be seen hunting over
North Valley during the day.
Photo Brian Hewitt

Left: **Curlew (*Numenius arquata*)**
Numbers of breeding Curlew on Skomer
have declined year on year, in 2016 the
population was lower than ever previously
recorded. Photo Mike Alexander

Right: **Carrion Crow (*Corvus corone*) Eggs and Chicks** A few pairs of Carrion Crows nest on rocks and in bushes on Skomer, the red-gaped chicks eagerly awaiting their parents returning with food. Photos Jane Matthews, Juan Brown

Whether it be trilling skylarks, the silent swoop of a short-eared owl or swarming puffins at dusk, Skomer's birding spectacle attracts the novice and professional alike.

Top: **Day visitors** Photo Jeff Morgan

Above: **Great Black-backed Gull (*Larus marinus*)** Photo Dave Boyle

Right: **Wheeling Puffins at South Haven** Throughout the breeding season thousands of Puffins whirl around their colonies at dusk on what seem like giant invisible carousels. Photo Dave Boyle

Above: **Great Black-backed Gull (*Larus marinus*)** The largest of the gulls and main predator of seabirds and Rabbits, there were nearly 300 pairs of Great Blackbacked Gulls on Skomer in the 1960s. Species control, compounded by an outbreak of botulism, caused a population crash in the 1970s. Numbers have been generally increasing since the mid 1980s and there have been up to 120 pairs in recent years. Photo Dave Boyle

Above: **Lesser Black-backed Gull (*Larus fuscus*)** Photo Chris Perrins

Left: **Herring Gull (*Larus argentatus*)** The three species of large gull are identified primarily by their back and leg colour. Great Black-backed Gulls are significantly larger than the other two. Photo Jason Moss

Right: **Peregrine Falcon (*Falco peregrinus*)** Peregrines have increased nationally from the low point of insecticide poisoning in the 1950s and 1960s. Skomer now holds about three cliff-nesting pairs. Photo Juan Brown

Below: **Guillemot (*Uria aalge*)** Guillemots have increased dramatically on Skomer in recent decades from a low point of 2,300 individuals in 1970 to almost 25,000 in 2016. Photo Dave Boyle

Left: **Snowmen** Photo Juan Brown

Right: **Ian the Chef** During the rebuilding project between 2005 and 2007 up to 30 builders stayed in temporary accommodation at the Old Farm. Feeding them all was Ian's job! The old volunteer facilities were replaced in 2006.
Photo Jane Matthews

Below: **Skomer Arms** Photo Emily Sharp

Display

Skomer – above and below water – is the stage for a kaleidoscopic display of changing colours and patterns throughout the year. The breathtaking carpets of Bluebells that bloom across the island in May are replaced by swathes of Red Campion in June. It's carnival time with no holds barred as the flora and fauna spring to life and show off their wares. Courting Razorbills, black and white on sun-baked guano, tip back their heads to display mustard-gold mouths.

Above right: **Bluebells Towards the Garland Stone** Photo Juan Brown

Right: **Red Campion (*Silene dioica*) at Welsh Way** Photo Jane Matthews

Puffins in full breeding regalia parade on the cliff-tops with neighbours and mates.

Socialising Puffins
Puffins at The Wick are exceptionally tame and can be watched at very close quarters. Photo Brian Hewitt

Below the waves, rare sea fans, kelp and soft corals waft in the currents of the Gulf Stream and diving seabirds, silvered by thousands of tiny air bubbles, plunge past in search of food.

Left: **Diving Puffins** Photo David Miller

Above: **Spiral Tube Worm (*Bispira volunicornis*)** Photo Philip Newman (MCZ)

Right: **Elegant Anemone (*Sagartia elegans*)** Photo Kate Lock (MCZ)

Specialist adaptations maximise potential for feeding beneath the waves. Puffins can dive to up to 60m in search of fish, while the feathery arms of the tube worm waft food down into its central mouth.

When magical creatures surface from the depths they provide a glimpse of another wilderness, a reminder that there is so much more that goes on unseen.

Left: **Grey Seal** Photo Mike Alexander

Above: **Common Dolphins** Marine mammals are resident around the island all year. Porpoises and (occasionally) dolphins can be spotted off the west coast of the island, breaking the surface of the water. Grey Seals haul out at

The Garland Stone and on Rye Rocks at low tide, particularly during the breeding and moulting seasons in spring and autumn. Up to 200 seals can also haul out to sleep on North Haven beach at these times. Photo Lyndon Lomax

With butterflies flip-flapping over the Bracken, moths and dragonflies perched below, there are spectacular displays of colour, shape and detail at every turn.

Above: **Scarlet Tiger Moth (*Callimorpha dominula*)** Photo Dave Boyle

Above right: **Emperor Moth (*Saturnia pavonia*)** Both these day-flying moths occur in small numbers on the island at different times of the year. Moth traps are set regularly to monitor nocturnal species. Photo Dave Boyle

Right: **Migrant Hawker (_Aeshna mixta_)** Migrating dragonflies appear in small but regular numbers throughout August and September. Photo Dave Boyle

This dainty and elusive moth feeds on flowering thrift, and is seen only on the calmest of warm summer days. An artificial pheromone, however, can tempt it into a frenzied mating display.

Left: **Thrift Clearwing (*Bembecia muscaeformis*)**

Above: **Flowering Thrift**
Photos Dave Boyle

Left: **Feather Star (*Antedon bifida*) and Painted Top Shell (*Callistoma zizyphinum*)** Feather Stars are from the same group of animals as the starfish called the Echinoderms. They have 10 featherlike arms with side branches that are used to hang onto the rock. The arms are used to filter food from the water and then transferred down a groove to the central mouth. Photo Kate Lock (MCZ)

Above: **The Old Farm** In Skomer's maritime climate snow is a rare phenomenon. Photo Mike Alexander

Right: **Autumn at The Wick**
Photo Jane Matthews

Far right: **North Haven**
Photo Jane Matthews

As the days shorten towards autumn Skomer's fields of Bracken die back, transforming the island into a fiery tangle of copper. Colourful seabirds are long gone but the ever-changing weather maintains the kaleidoscopic scene.

Left: **Jessie's Window** For volunteers stepping out of their daily lives and into an experience so close to the natural world, the island can have a marked effect on their direction and way of seeing. Photo Amber Rowlands

Right: **Barn Owl (*Tyto alba*) feather** In 2004 a pair of Barn Owls nested in the workshop at the Old Farm and successfully reared two young. This was first breeding record for the species on Skomer since the late nineteenth century. Photo Richard Brown

Beauty is not just confined to open vistas and the conventional elements of wildlife on Skomer. It can be found and appreciated in all things, dead and alive.

Routine

Skomer is a well-established outpost of ecological study and surveillance with longstanding links to Oxford and Sheffield Universities. Researchers spend up to four months on the island each season, building an accurate picture of the health and prosperity of each individual species and the island as a whole.

Right: **Haul-out at Matthew's Wick**
Monitoring of the Grey Seal breeding population has been taking place on Skomer since 1983. Photo Jane Matthews

A Voluntary Warden scheme provides the facility for between four and six people to stay on the island for a week at a time during the season. Their help is central to the running of the reserve and duties include monitoring, path clearing, general maintenance and visitor management. It is a perfect way to experience the island, its wildlife and the magic of being one of the few to remain after the last boat load of visitors has left at the end of the day.

Above left: **Volunteers** Each year approximately 50% of Skomer's volunteers are newcomers, others return again and again. Of the many veterans Dr. Bill Dixon (right) first volunteered in 1968. Photo Jane Matthews

Above: **Manx Shearwater Chick** In a warm burrow a Manx Shearwater egg will be incubated by each of its parents in turn, for approximately 51 days. Once hatched the chick will continue to live below ground for about a further 69 days during which time it can grow to be twice the weight of an adult. These fat reserves will be essential to the bird's survival after fledging, on its first migratory passage to South America. Photos Juan Brown

While nature is generally left to take its course, data are collected from every corner of the island.

Above: **South Haven and The Neck**
The Neck remains off limits to the general public, only accessed when necessary by staff and researchers for monitoring purposes. This offers a control by which to gauge the human impact on the rest of the island. Photo Bob Ball

Below: **Double Cliff Shore Monitoring**
Double Cliff is the steepest of the shores studied in the Skomer MCZ shore monitoring programme. The challenge is to collect the data and take photos of the sample areas by suspending quadrats from a rope attached to pitons whilst floating in a boat – a task only attempted in calm conditions. Photo Kate Lock (MCZ)

Seabird species are monitored fastidiously each year, forming an invaluable picture of the health of the wider marine environment. With pressures on our seas from commercial fishing and climate change such monitoring is becoming increasingly important.

Left: **The Amos**

Right: **Ringed Guillemot**
As part of a long-term productivity and survivorship study by Sheffield University, three hundred chicks and as many adults as possible are ringed each year. This bird was ringed in 2001. Photos Dave Boyle

Above: **Species Monitoring** Sheffield
University's Field Assistant spends four
months a year studying one colony of
Guillemots on the west coast of the island
- a dream job for Elisa Miquel Riera in
2017. Photo Jason Moss

Above: **Razorbill Chick** Photo Jason Moss

Right: **Marked Seal Pup** For over 35 years a census of the Grey Seal breeding population has been carried out, recording as many as 200 pups born per season, scattered over the many remote coves and beaches of the island. Pups are given a colour-coded spray mark at the base of their backs so their progress can be monitored from afar until they shed their first coat at about three weeks old. Photos Jane Matthews

Protection, understanding and education are fundamental to the success of the Reserve.

Left: **Geolocator** Researchers from Oxford University fit tiny data loggers to Manx Shearwaters. By recording time of sunrise and day length, the position of a bird can be determined on its long transatlantic migration to South America during the non-breeding season. Photo Dave Boyle

Right: **Rebuilding the Hide** Voluntary Wardens are valuable to the island in so many ways. In 2016 Dave and Geoff helped rebuild the Moory Mere hide. Photo Jason Moss

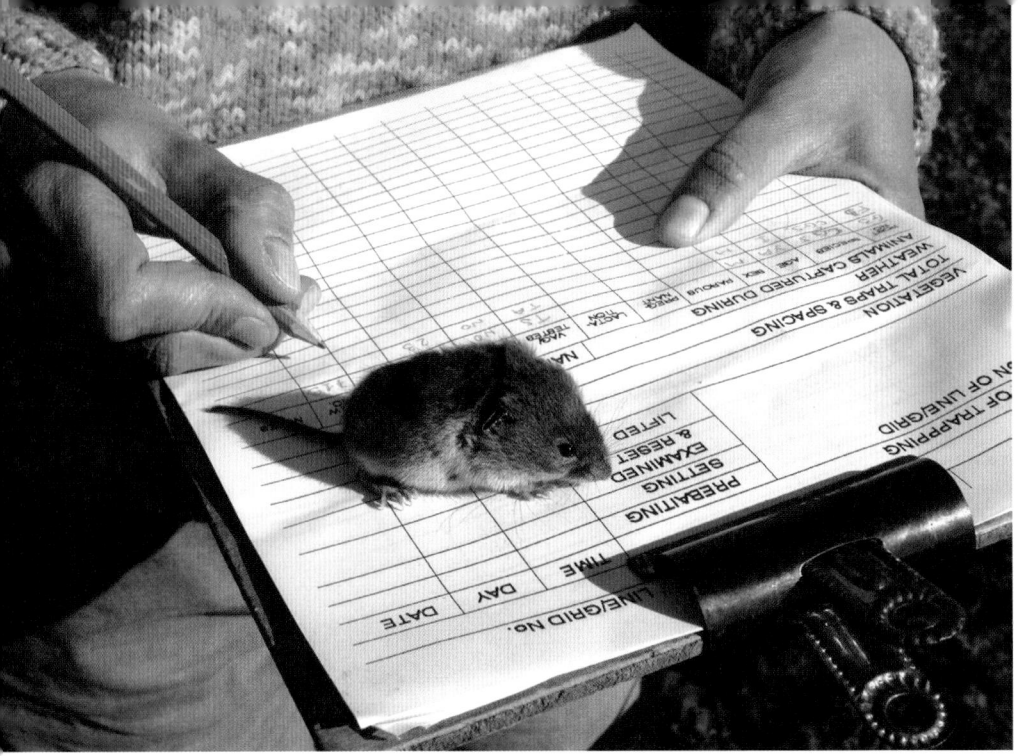

All creatures, resident or visiting, make their mark on Skomer's history in so many different ways. This is what makes it such a fascinating place to be.

Above: **Island Vole Census** The Skomer Vole (*Clethrionomys glareolus skomerensis*) is a subspecies of the Bank Vole unique to the island. Every 10 years a whole island survey is carried out to determine the island's population. In 2005 it was estimated to be between 4 and 10,000, a drop from over 20,000 in the previous decade. Photo Tim Healing

Above: **Tim Healing** Tim has been returning to Skomer for over 45 years to monitor the vole population. The skills and equipment needed for his day job as a humanitarian aid worker in some of the most challenging countries on earth often come in handy on the island and he is famous for his breathtaking array of small gadgets. Photo Juan Brown

Left: **Jean Betteridge (1927-2007)** There is no upper age limit for volunteering on Skomer. Jean first came to the island in her late seventies. Photo Juan Brown

Busy with day visitors six days a week leaves only Monday, when the island is closed, for essential maintenance, monitoring and a spot of relaxation.

Left: **Cliff Counts** Each year counts are made of all the species breeding on Skomer. This can involve hours and hours of observation from the water. Photo Jason Moss

Above: **Cricket** It's not all hard work on a National Nature Reserve. A tradition of island cricket matches has grown over the years but in 2005 Skomer's team were left bewildered by a superior Mainland team! Photo Jane Matthews

Above: **Visitors leaving the Island**
For staff and volunteers many of the duties
revolve around the day visitors, their safety
and ensuring that all who come onto the
island make it off on the boat at the end of
the day. Photo Jeff Morgan

Right: **Evening over North Valley**
Photo Jane Matthews

On Skomer there's no such thing as a 9 to 5. Away from the social structures that punctuate life on the mainland, island time is defined largely by seasons and the setting sun.

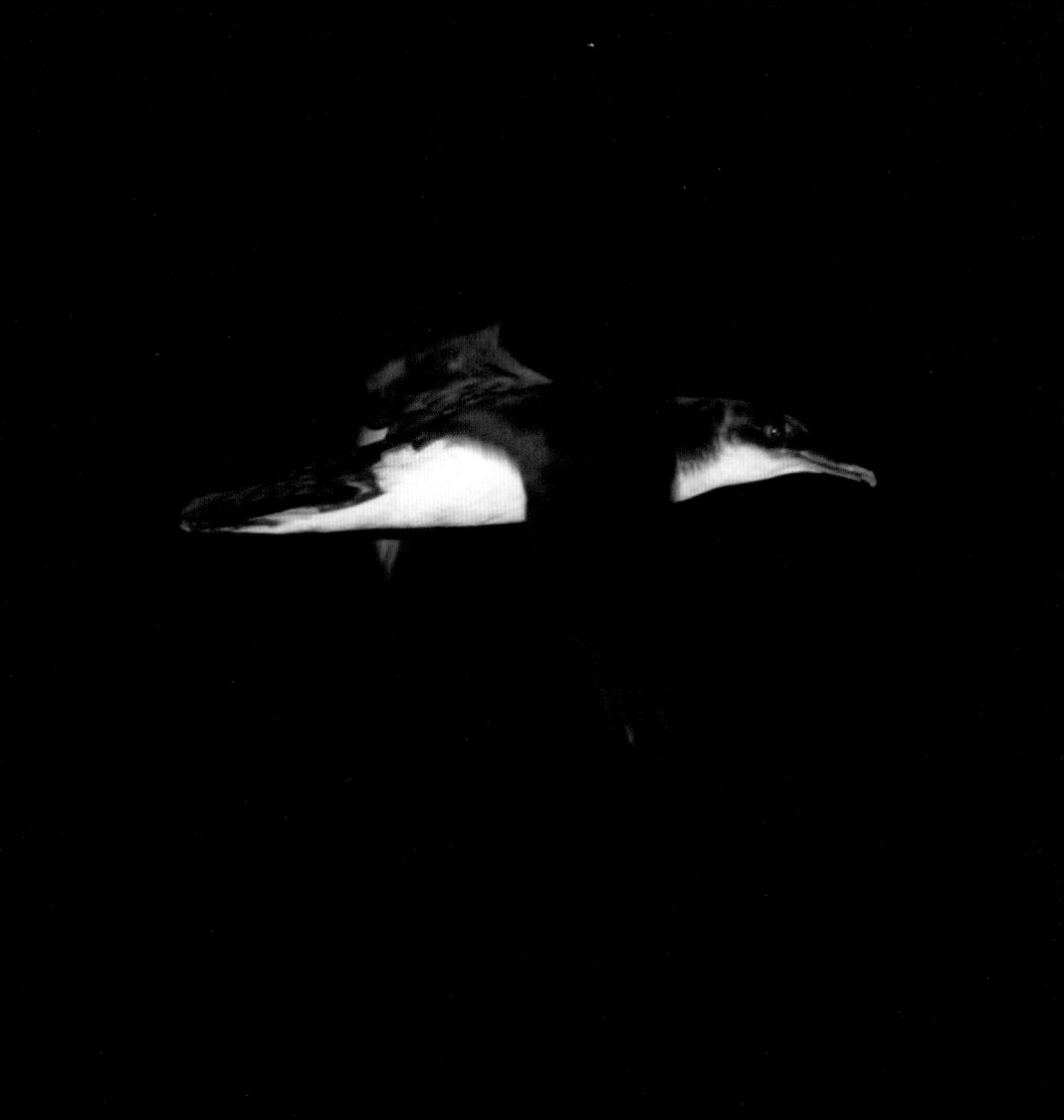

Nightlife

As night falls and streets across the mainland flicker with the glow of television, the sky above Skomer starts to flutter and whirr with the return of the Manx Shearwater.

Skomer has the largest single colony of Manx Shearwaters anywhere in the world. These birds fly over seven thousand miles on their migratory passage to South America and find their way back each year to this tiny tip of Wales to breed.

Built for a life at sea with legs set far back on its body, the shearwater is unable to move on land with either grace or precision. It returns to land only in complete darkness to avoid falling prey to the Great Black-backed Gull.

Indoors another Skomer ritual begins... Bird Log has taken place almost nightly throughout the seasons since 1960. All the island's residents convene to record all the day's sightings. Bird Log's testimony lies in the volumes of data that form an invaluable record of seasonal and long-term changes in numbers of birds and other wildlife.

Page 132/133 and above: **Manx Shearwater** The Manx Shearwater relies on complete darkness for its return to land to avoid predation by the Great Black-backed Gull. Moonlit nights spell danger; if they must return to the burrow they do so as swiftly and quietly as possible. Photos Brian Hewitt and Dave Boyle

Left: **Moonlit Bluebells** Photo Flora Moody

During the day shearwaters
that are not on eggs feed far
out to sea. At dusk they raft
in huge numbers waiting to
return to land after dark.

Left: **Manx Shearwaters at Sea**
Shearwaters can embark on long distance fishing trips for up to seven days while the partner bird remains below ground. Recent tagging has shown, contrary to previous belief, that feeding birds head north into the Irish Sea as far as the Mull of Kintyre. Photo Lyndon Lomax

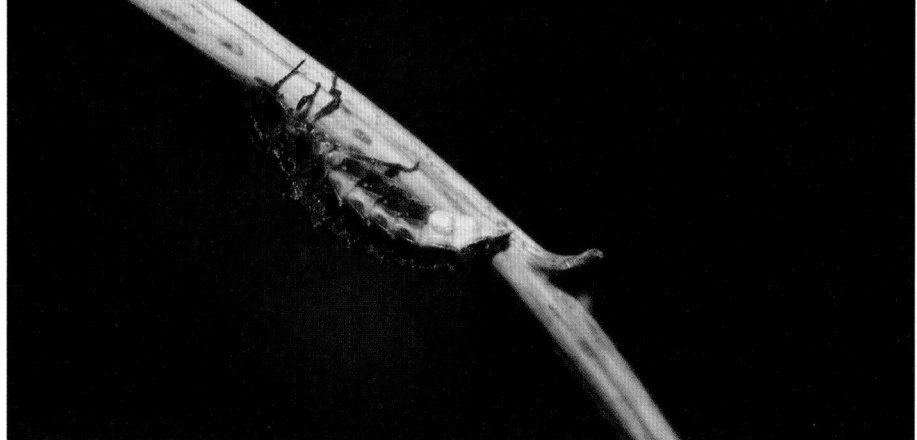

The festival of sound and light continues until just before dawn. With the most dazzling array of costumes, the island's nocturnal species threaten to upstage their daytime counterparts.

Left: **Puffin below ground** Puffin activity often peaks at dusk, when chicks are below ground, and then again at dawn. But little is known about their activities throughout the night. Photo Richard Brown

Above: **Glow-worm (*Lampyris noctiluca*)**

Right: **European Storm Petrel (*Hydrobates pelagicus*)** Glow-worms often light up the track from North Haven on summer nights. The secretive Storm Petrel breeds in a few remote boulder beaches on the island and, like the shearwaters, only returns at night. Photos Dave Boyle

Above: **Night Flight** Photo Jane Matthews

Right: **Outside its Burrow** The highest concentration of shearwaters is found at North Haven and, on a dark or foggy night, the sky is filled with incoming birds, calling to their partners below ground. Breeders and non-breeders alike litter the banks and the lights of the mainland serve only to remind that it is near, yet very, very far. Photo Dave Boyle

Nothing compares to the ghostly sight and sound of the Manx Shearwaters' return. It is the largest colony anywhere in the world and the only easily accessible place in Britain to witness such a spectacle.

Bird Log
by Jeremy Grange

Above and right: Bird Log
Photos Jane Matthews

The pencil-point hovers
above the page's horizon,
lifting for a moment from its hunt

as latecomers, breathing apology,
steal in from the twilight's
pendent stillness.

You resume the broken chant
and words take flight:
guillemot and gannet, cormorant, chough.

This nightly vigil embraces
the island. A final roll-call
before sleep, testing the textures

of presence and absence:
travellers, visitors,
fixtures and departures.

In the bubble of light, fed
by the generator's heartbeat,
stories unfold like butterflies:

the migrant, displaced and lost,
a stained glass ornament
pressed against the window;

the cow seal, heaving herself
over rocks to rid the beach of you, your
rout
reflected in her pup's gibbous eyes;

a sunfish – monstrous, incomplete –
hove-to and helpless in the sound.
You log each memory with a tick.

Outside, the choking, half-mad calls
kick-start as young shearwaters
launch into another night

of short-lived flight and clumsy crash-
landings.
Some sit at the burrow's lip,
blinking in the half-moonlight,

while they absorb the stars' imprint,
calculate the constellations' skew.
For soon, they'll be gone –

suddenly, impossibly proficient,
skimming the Earth's curve
like skipped stones across sea.

And you too will depart for the mainland,
leaving the wintering island
to mark you absent.

As islanders wend their way
back to their beds by torchlight
they dodge shearwaters, frogs
and toads. On a damp night
the paths can be littered with
all three.

Left: **Common Toad (*Bufo bufo*)**
Photo Richard Brown

Above: **Common Frog (*Rana temporaria*)**
Skomer has an unusually high density of
frogs and toads, and an especially orange
form of Common Frog. Both can be seen
in large numbers on the tracks in wet
weather. Photo Dave Boyle

Just before dawn the island falls quiet and the night's secrets get hidden away. All that remain are the discarded wings of those that didn't survive; bodies stripped clean by the gulls.

Left: **Dawn on the West Coast**
Photo Bob Ball

Above: **Carcass** Photo Emily Sharp

"...the quite smooth sea turned again in its perpetual come and go, and took us slowly back in so many hours, till we found ourselves again by evening where we had started, at the mouth of Jack Sound."
Hilaire Belloc, *The Cruise of the Nona* (1925).

Above: **Skomer from the West**
Left: **South of The Neck**
Photos Jane Matthews

Skomer's Natural History

440 million years ago, during the Silurian geological period, volcanic activity laid down the sequence of rocks that forms Skomer today. This sequence extends out from the Marloes Peninsula on the mainland to Middleholm, Skomer, Grassholm, and out to the Smalls – a group of islets about 22 km to the west. Erosion of surrounding softer rocks and fault activity isolated these hard rocky outposts, creating islands, the biggest and most accessible of which is Skomer.

The characteristic, relatively flat-topped 'tableland' was created by marine activity when Skomer was underwater between 80 and 90 million years ago. Upon this, a deep soil cap has formed which provides sanctuary for the burrow-nesting Puffin and Manx Shearwater. The surrounding sea forms a barrier to land predators. Skomer is the biggest Puffin colony in southern Britain (approximately

25,000 birds) while the 300,000 pairs of Manx Shearwater represent a significant proportion of the entire world population. This species is particular about where it nests, requiring soil in which to burrow, a lack of land predators, access to rich feeding grounds, and enough darkness to allow a safe return from a day's fishing (so northern latitudes that stay light during the summer are unsuitable); Skomer fits the bill on all counts.

Above ground a thick vegetation has developed. In mid-late May Bluebells form dense tracts. This species has a global distribution limited to the Atlantic coast of Europe. As the Bluebells wither in June, Bracken takes over, forming a shady canopy akin to the woodland that Bluebells are normally associated with. Amongst the vegetation nests a large colony of Lesser Black-backed Gulls, forming a significant percentage of the world's population of the race graelsii.

The vertical igneous cliffs on the edge of this island plateau provide safe inaccessible ledges for other nesting seabirds: the Kittiwake, a strictly-marine gull which sticks a cup of mud and grass to the rock in which to lay its eggs; Guillemot – a penguin-like bird which does not even bother to build a nest, laying a single cone-shaped egg on bare rock, huddled together with thousands of its own; and Razorbill, present on Skomer in internationally important numbers.

Skomer provides a haven for Grey Seals – present all year and pupping in the autumn – while its isolation has resulted in the evolution of its own race of Bank Vole, the unique Skomer Vole.

Having been legally protected for over 50 years, Skomer hosts a wealth of wildlife, its relative accessibility has enabled conservationists, scientists and the general public to study and enjoy this national treasure without compromising the flora and fauna which make it so special.
Juan Brown

Designations at a glance:

- National Nature Reserve
- Site of Special Scientific Interest
- Marine Conservation Zone
- Special Protection Area (European)
- Scheduled Ancient Monument
- Geological Conservation Review site
- Within Pembrokeshire Marine Special Area of Conservation (European)
- Within Pembrokeshire Coast National Park

Contributors

Jane Matthews

Jane Matthews was born in Bristol, studied Fine Art at Oxford University and Art History at The Courtauld Institute in London. She was working as an artist in the TV and film industry in London when she first went to Skomer as a volunteer and met Juan, the Warden. She moved to Skomer to live with Juan in 2003, working on the Grey Seal Breeding Census, writing and taking photographs.

Their daughter Martha was born in 2005 and in 2007 all three left Skomer for Shetland, at the northern tip of the UK. Still based in Shetland, Jane works as an illustrator and exhibition manager.

Iolo Williams

Iolo Williams was born and brought up in mid Wales and, having studied for a degree in ecology in London, returned to Wales to work for the RSPB. He spent nearly 15 years as Species Officer for Wales, working on a wide range of different birds, including Black Grouse, Hen Harrier, Red Kite, Chough and Lapwing. He left the organisation in 1998 to work full-time in the media. As well as broadcasting, Iolo has written several books on wildlife in both Welsh and English. He is a keen sportsman, is married to Ceri and has two boys, Dewi and Tomos.

Matthew Parris

Matthew Parris was born and educated in South Africa, Cyprus, Rhodesia and Swaziland. He has been a civil servant, an MP, a television presenter, a journalist and radio broadcaster. He has led expeditions to the Sahara, South America and the Andes, spent the winter on Kerguelen (Desolation Island) in the Southern Ocean, among albatross, penguins and elephant seals, and (for BBC Radio 4) followed camel trains from the highlands of Ethiopia into the inferno of the Danakil depression on their ancient route to collect salt. He visited Skomer while making a radio series about animal migration.

David Miller

Born in Lancashire in 1966, David Miller now lives and works in the heart of the west Wales countryside, in a wooded valley near the Taf and Towy estuaries with the dramatic Pembrokeshire coastline on his doorstep. He paints mostly British wildlife, usually in oils, travelling widely to gather reference and inspiration for his work.
www.davidmillerart.co.uk

Brian Hewitt

From an early age I have had a deep interest in wildlife and, later on, photography. Skomer is one of those special places that gets its hooks in to you. If I'd known about the volunteering I think I would have done it a long time ago.

Lyndon Lomax

After 30 years with British Gas, based in the Midlands, the move to Pembrokeshire was made in 1997. Since then visiting the Islands, the cliff tops, and off shore boat trips have been almost a daily occurrence both to study and enjoy the marine life available to us. If my enthusiasm and some of my pictures excite others to enjoy the wonders of our coastal birds and marine life then my time here will have been more than well spent.

Jeff Morgan

Jeff is a Wales-based photojournalist whose work appears in publications worldwide.

Juan Brown

Juan Brown was Warden of Skomer between 1999 and 2008, having come from the Farne Islands in Northumberland via the Isle of Noss, Shetland. He returned to Shetland with partner Jane and daughter Martha, and works for Scottish Natural Heritage.

Jeremy Grange
Jeremy Grange is a BBC radio producer based in Wales and has made several programmes about Skomer. 'Bird Log' was inspired by a visit to the island to recording a programme about Manx Shearwaters. The poem won *BBC Wildlife* Magazine's Poet of the Year Competition.

Emily Sharp
My first Skomer experience was as a volunteer in 2002 and I returned time and again to take photographs. What I most love about Skomer is its wild, magical landscape, Bird Log and falling asleep to the deathly cries of the Manx Shearwaters. I caught the island bug and gave up my London life in 2007, moving to Shetland where I now work in the arts, sing classical music and continue to take photographs.

Bob Ball
I first came to Skomer in 1986 and have been every year since. For nearly 20 years I volunteered for a week – maybe two – on the island. During those wonderful times I introduced my wife, family and friends to an experience they will never forget: living and working with wildlife on a paradise island. Nowadays I have a bear for company who writes his own stories for his own blog: Mindfully Bertie. He has already written about Skomer and Skokholm.

Dave Boyle
Dave Boyle worked as a researcher on Skomer for several years. He studied seabird populations as part of a longstanding study by the Edward Grey Institute (Oxford University) and the Grey Seal population for Natural Resources Wales. Since leaving Skomer he has worked in New Zealand on the Chatham Island Taiko recovery programme.

Chris Perrins
Professor at Oxford University and eminent ornithologist, Chris Perrins has been supervising the research work of the Edward Grey Institute of Ornithology on Skomer for over 40 years.

Tim Healing
Tim Healing is a humanitarian aid worker who has spent a lot of time abroad in some rather dodgy places. He did his PhD on Skomer voles starting in 1970 and now visits the island annually as part of a long term study of the voles. He says it keeps him (fairly) sane.

Mike Alexander
Mike Alexander's passion for conservation began as a boy when he first visited Skomer. He eventually became Warden in 1976 and the ten years he spent there confirmed everything he believed about the importance of nature conservation. From 1991-2008 he had overall responsibility for the NNR series in Wales and since then has been the Chairman of PONT, an organisation forging links between farmers and nature conservation. He teaches at Bangor University and Birkbeck, London, and is a trustee of The Wildlife Trust of South & West Wales.

Amber Rowlands
Photographer Amber Rowlands was first introduced to Skomer by her stepfather, Bob, and stayed as a volunteer with her sister, Jessie. Neither she nor Jessie knew what to expect, having never done volunteering work before. It was an incredible experience for both of them and life changing for Jessie. Amber's work has appeared in *The Observer*, *the Telegraph*, *Le Monde* and *Time*, as well as several style and design magazines.

Richard Brown
Richard Brown was Assistant Warden on Skomer from 2005 to 2007. He has lived on Welsh islands for every subsequent seabird season and, with his partner Giselle, has wardened Skokholm for the last six years. In the British winter they visit seabird islands around the world, helping with projects such as eradicating rats on Caribbean islands and translocating albatrosses.

MCZ
The Skomer Marine Conservation Zone is managed by Natural Resouces Wales. The photos are a collection by the MCZ team and long term volunteers; Philip Newman, Kate Lock, Blaise Bullimore, Rob Gibbs, Mark Burton, Vicki Howe, Rohan Holt, Jennifer Jones.

Alison Hayes (left) and **Flora Moody** (right)
Alison Hayes is an artist and writer. She inspired new ideas and directions in the course of wildlife preservation and how people perceive art through her body of artwork based on and around Skomer and Grassholm Islands.

Flora Moody was Alison's assistant on Skomer.

Jason Moss
I have been working on Skomer Island since 2014, as Assistant Warden and then, last year, as Seabird Fieldworker for Gloucester University. It has been a pleasure to meet so many wonderful and inspirational people over the years, while being surrounded daily by incredible wildlife. As is the case for many people who get the 'Skomer bug', I know I will return many times in the future!

Additional photographs by **Tim Guilford, Ben Dean, David Milborrow , Robert Bush** and **Birgitta Büche.**

Index